Excuse Me,
(I Burped)

Achieving Your Very Best by Learning
the Secrets of Good Manners
& Common Courtesy

RONALD J. SCARIANO

ISBN: 1456477153
ISBN-13: 9781456477158

To Mom and Dad with love.
You taught me the difference between right and wrong,
good and bad and dumb and dumber. But the most important
lesson you bestowed on me was in caring for others it is
impossible to give more than you receive.

Table of Contents

Forward

One night at the dinner table our oldest daughter Samantha, let out a thundering, roof rattling, fog horn sounding belch that was so gross that it would have made a yak herder blush.

Samantha, a sophomore in high school at the time, knew better but because her mother and younger sister laughed (...and, o.k., I smiled), she decided that this was acceptable behavior and did it again the next night.

Ah, therein lies the dilemma for a young person. Should I get the quick hit of shallow acceptance by making people laugh with unacceptable behavior or should I strive for the inner confidence that comes from good manners.

What follows are some simple thoughts on achieving your very best, through good manners and common courtesy.

Baseball Caps

(or any hat)

Baseball type caps are great for showing your support for your favorite team ("Go 49ers!") or to express your feelings (such as FDNY). They can even be worn in such a way that shows you are an individual, such as wearing your cap backwards...which of course negates one of the major advantages of the cap, which is to have the bill of the cap protect your eyes from the sun. But hey you're an individual, you seek your own way, you chart your own course, you wear your hat backwards. Why? Because everyone else does.

When *not* to wear a baseball cap, or any other cap or hat.

1. When you are inside any building, restaurant, theater, etc. *But especially never in a private home.*
2. Inside a church.
3. Or honoring our flag.
4. When you greet an adult, especially a lady.

To wear a baseball cap in any of these situations is;

A. Rude
B. Disrespectful
C. Lowers your I.Q. by at least 40 points.
(The rules for cap/hats pertain to males. Females get a "pass" on this one).

1

Phone Manners

When calling another person the correct opening is "hi, this is (<u>your name)</u>, may I please speak with (<u>name of the person you would like to speak with</u>)?

"Is Charlie there" or "Get me Charlie" is rude and shows lack of manners.

Sometimes you will be asked to take a message. Be sure to get all the information; name, date, reason for call and most important the *correct phone number!* My secretary one time gave me a message that said "Bill called" and then had written down six numbers (there are seven in a normal local phone number). When I asked her what the seventh phone number was she said she thought I would know. I didn't. When I said, "...who is Bill?" she said, "Bill said, you'd know". I didn't.

A cell phone is a wonderful convenience. However just like a car, a baseball bat or a water hose, in the hands of the wrong person a cell phone can be a real annoyance.

We all know you are important. You must be important, after all you have a cell phone. However, believe it or not, no one much cares to hear your phone conversation. Take it out of the crowd and into a private place.

Finally, think about this; when you're on the phone and you hear the click that tells you, you have another phone call coming in, how do you think the person that you say, "hold for a minute, I have another call coming in", feels? How would you feel? Maybe like you're second best, not very important, or that the person you're holding for is hoping for a better deal. Any way you cut it, it is not a very polite way to handle a phone call.

It's "yes" not "yeah"

Have you ever noticed how much nicer it is to hear someone say "yes" rather than "yeah"? Do you prefer hearing "yes" rather than "ah- huh"? How about "no" rather than "ah-ah" or "naaa"?

Now this may seem like a very small item. In fact it is a very small item. However in business there is a saying that if you will take care of the little things the big things will take care of themselves. Developing good manners is the same way.

Table Manners

Recently our daughter raved about a new friend she had made in school. This new friend was a straight "A" student, an actress, piano player, singer and had gotten a varsity "letter" in sports her freshman year. My daughter not only "gushed" when she spoke of her new friend, but she also seemed to be slightly intimidated by her. However, after one meal at our home, whereby my daughter's friend put her elbows on the table, talked with her mouth full, dipped her head to within 3 inches of the plate and ate at the speed of sound, my daughter was not quite as impressed with her new friend. She wasn't intimidated anymore by her either.

You may not realize it, but when you are eating with other people, they are noticing how you eat. Like it or not you are making a lasting impression about the quality of person you are, without saying a word (although, unfortunately your mouth may be open!).

Why not;

1. Sit up straight.
2. Take small bites.
3. Keep your arms off the table.
4. Don't talk with your mouth full of food.

5. I would also say don't talk with your mouth full of liquid, but when you think about it, that situation would probably take care of itself.
6. Chew with your mouth closed.

If you will follow these 6 thoughts you will make it a much more enjoyable dining experience for everyone at the table.

Speak!

Nothing is quite as annoying as watching a friend's or neighbor's child grow from the toddling years to that of a teenager and find that as an adult you are now invisible to that teenager. You can be a rascal and a scoundrel, but much will be forgiven by an adult if you greet them with a friendly smile and a warm "hello".

How do you know if they see you? Real simple, if you see them, they can (and do!) see you. Speak!

PS. As my mother used to say, "…you'll never get even if you stop speaking". Always speak, even if you're mad at someone. It will keep them guessing and drive them nuts.

Being a Gentleman, Take 1

A gentleman always walks on the outside of a lady. There are several legends as to why this is. One is that, in the olden days, if a horse got loose in the street a gentleman could protect the lady from the galloping hoofs. Another legend (probably from the East Coast), is that a gentleman always walks on the outside of a lady, to shield her from any garbage that is thrown out the above windows. Wherein lies the truth is of little matter. A gentleman always walks on the outside of a lady.

Guidelines for a Gentleman:

1. A gentleman always helps a lady on/off with her coat.

2. A gentleman always allows a lady to enter a building, subway, elevator, etc., first.

3. A gentleman always opens the door for a lady.

4. A gentleman is always admired and desired by a lady.

Being a Gentleman, Take 2

Whenever a lady and/or an adult enters a room it is proper for a gentleman to stand (and remove your hat, which of course you should have already done when you enter any building).

A gentleman never shakes hands with **anyone**, while he is seated.

A gentleman never shakes hand with a lady, *unless the lady first offers her hand.*

A handshake should be firm and strong, but not hurtful or over powering. It is a sign that you have come in peace, and that you have no weapon to harm another person. Don't ruin it by doing a take off on a "standing arm wrestling" instead of just shaking hands.

Even more distressing than a too strong handshake is a "limp fish" sort of a handshake that leaves the other person looking at you like you are a wet Bass or a just cooked noodle.

Remember, as it has been said many times, you never get a second chance to make a first impression.

Thank You Notes/
Christmas Cards

Whenever a gift, or a kindness (such as a meal), is given, it is proper to handwrite a thank you note. Never, never, get a pre-printed thank you note and simply sign your name.

While we are on the subject, every year at Christmas time I get mad. In fact when I get this Christmas card I often jump up and down, say a word that I shouldn't, rip the card apart and throw it in the garbage. Why? Because it is a printed Christmas card that they "assembly lined". The envelope is addressed in the wife's handwriting. The stamp is crooked, so I know his young daughter put it on. Then the final holiday touch is the husband has signed it, Fred, Helen and the kids.

Not only is it very impersonal, as they don't even know who is getting the card, but I have not seen or talked to these people for a year. How about a little information. The wife got a new job, the family got a new car and junior has finally graduated with honors from reform school.

To send any card that is pre-printed, that you simply sign your name to, is a waste of your time and an insult to the person you sent it to.

Chewing Gum

Chewing gum in public with your mouth closed is improper. Chewing gum in public with your mouth open is worse. You look like a cow.

Although many people eat in their cars or walking down the street, my grandmother would have never done that. She said the reason she didn't do it is because there might be someone watching you that does not have the money to eat, at least the money to eat that ice cream cone or candy bar. She did not want to hurt anyone's feelings or make anyone feel left out. My grandmother was a very sweet lady.

Eating

It is considered very poor form to start eating before the entire table has been seated and everyone has been served. Likewise, it is very rude to leave the table before everyone is finished with their meal.

If you must leave the table before everyone is finished it is proper to ask, "may I please be excused, I have to (fill in the reason)."

Only those brought up in a cave by wild animals would consider eating with their arms on the table, or speaking with their mouth full of food. Only if you are sure that the roof leaks (and it coming down so hard that chipmunks are surfing in the drive way) should you wear a hat of any kind while eating at home, school, a friends house, a restaurant and yes even a picnic.

Gossip

Ben Franklin said, "I will speak all the good I know of everyman, and none of the evil I know of any man".

Ben may have been bald, fat and funny looking, but he really has a point there, doesn't he?

Before you share that juicy piece of gossip ask your self;

1. Is it true, or do I just assume it is true because I heard it from someone else?
2. Will telling this "story" help anyone?
3. If I were the person in the story, would I want people talking about me?

Friends share thoughts, goals, ideas and experiences. Friends don't share gossip.

Honor

My second grade teacher, Mrs. Worley told my class, over 50 years ago, "...a true test of a person's honor, is what that person would do if they knew for certain, no one would ever find out".

50+ years later, it is still a very good test of one's honor.

Never Lie, Cheat, or Steal

A lie for the liar is hard to remember. If it is the truth you will have no trouble remembering it. However something very strange happens when you tell a lie. The person you lied to can remember the lie. You can't. You'll get caught.

Cheating robs your soul. Forever you will remember that you broke your trust with yourself. You did less than you were able, but took credit for more than you actually did. Slowly, then faster and faster you will become disenchanted with the person looking back at you in the mirror each day.

Stealing undermines your confidence to achieve. When you steal you can rationalize it in many different ways. I needed it. The store owner charges too much anyway. They're rich, they won't miss it. But the bottom line is you took something that did not belong to you, that you could have had if you had worked for it.

Invitations

An invitation should be responded to immediately if at all possible. After all, your host/hostess is trying to plan an enjoyable event with you in mind. A person with manners will often surprise their host/hostess with a small "hostess" gift as a way of saying thank you. Of course a person with manners will not only say "thank you" but will also hand write a thank you note thanking their host/hostess for the invitation and the event as discussed earlier.

Never, never accept an invitation and then cancel because you *got a better offer.* This is not only very rude, but it also shows a weakness in your character.

Entering

No matter if you are entering a room, elevator, car or bus, always allow the people *out* before you step in. This is not only polite, it is also just common sense.

And while we are on the subject, a gentleman always offers his seat on the bus, train or any public situation to any female, child or elderly person.

It amazes me how often I see a male walk through a door way, walk down an aisle or move into a movie seat while the woman walks behind. A gentleman always allow a lady to enter first (unless of course there is a perceived risk of danger).

Listen

Everyone, including your parents, spouses, siblings, etc. want to be listened to. It does not matter if the other person is describing a dream, talking about a T.V. program or expounding on the phrase credited to Eli Whitney ("keep your cotton pickin' hands off my gin"). Be a good listener.

Look the person in the eye, (a little trick if you tend to be shy is to look at the other person's eye brows).

Do not interrupt. It can be tempting. Don't do it.

Ask questions about the subject rather than looking for the first opportunity to change the subject.

It is very difficult to look the person in the eye and ask intelligent questions about the subject at hand if you are watching T.V. or reading the newspaper. Give the speaker your complete attention.

Name

What is the most golden sound to every person on the planet? Their name. Learn it and use it! Remembering people's name is a strong compliment to that person. Remembering their name says that they are important to you.

Most people, when they are meeting someone for the first time are so concerned about saying their own name, that they completely forget the other person's name in a matter of seconds. Everyone has the ability to remember the other person's name. Here are a couple of hints on remembering the other person's name that will help you.

1. Listen when the person says their name. If you do not hear it ask the person to repeat it. (Repeat again, and again until you get it).
2. If it is a long or difficult name, ask the person to tell you about it's origin.
3. Use the name immediately in conversation. (As in, "... well Fred Abarkowitz, it is great to meet you").
4. Help the other person with your name. (Such as the name *Scariano*. Think "Scar" and then "piano" without the "p").

Be On Time

Being on time or being late is simply a habit that you establish. Establishing the habit of being late is rude, inconsiderate and egotistical. Establishing the habit of being on time demonstrates your consideration for others and your ability to manage your own life.

It is *not* acceptable to be late. However, don't compound the rudeness of being late, by not at least calling the person and letting them know you are going to be late.

Be Aware

Be aware of your surroundings. If you are in a non-smoking area, then don't smoke. If you are in an area that allows smoking I would still suggest you don't smoke, as it not only will kill you, but while you're alive it will make your breath stink and offend 70% of the people around you, even if they don't say anything.

If you are in a movie theater, don't talk when the program starts. Keep your feet off the chair in front of you. Someone in the future will be putting their head where you rested your feet.

If you see an old friend as you are entering a store, great! Greet them and catch up on old times. Just do it without blocking the door way.

Now that many airlines are no longer serving food, question if you should bring food on the airlines. It is still rude to eat in front of others even if they are strangers and even if you are on an airplane.

If you need help, the proper way to ask for it is by saying "…excuse me, would you please help me". Never demand help and snap your fingers or whistle to get someone's attention so they can help you.

Getting Attention

Many people try to get attention by being rude or acting boorish. Young people often revert to loud or obnoxious behavior to get attention. Teenage girls 40 years ago tried to get attention at sporting events (especially basketball games), by getting up and walking to the bathroom, phone or refreshment stand 8 to 12 times per game. That little ploy is still popular today!

The above type of attention getting behavior is not only rude and annoying but like a sugar cube in a shower, it just does not last that long.

Quality, long lasting attention is given to and kept by those that understand that good manners are common sense. Because, just as common sense is hardly common, good manners are rare and treasured when found.

Restaurant Manners

Always tip the breakfast server more than standard. Remember they had to get up, get *their breakfast,* shower and drive to work to serve you your breakfast.

Sometimes a server will introduce themselves to you ("Hi, I'm Betty and I will be serving you today"). In this case it is alright to call Betty...Betty! However it is **never** proper to;

1. Use an endearment such as "sweetie, honey, or hey baby".
2. Whistle or snap your fingers.
3. And it is completely against the law to in any way touch your server!

...and while we are on the subject of restaurant behavior, it seems that middle age or older men think that it is acceptable to "flirt" with a female server. It is not only not acceptable, you also look like an old fool.

Of course the waitress laughs at your remarks and smiles at you. She lives on your tips. But it certainly doesn't mean that she thinks you're funny, cute or desirable.

(Note: Tipping is a very personal matter, however here are a couple of thoughts on tipping)

Realize that:

A) Most servers depend on "tips" to live on.
B) Most restaurants look at "tips" as part of the server's pay and hence pay minimum wage or less.
C. The I.R.S in most cases demands that servers declare and pay taxes on a fixed amount of "tips" for each hour they work, regardless of what they actually made during those hours.
D. Bottom line is that it is still your money. If the server has done a poor job, you are not required to leave anything.

However, if the server has done a good job, been pleasant and prompt, it shows very poor form to not leave a tip of 15% or more of the total bill.

Smile

Yes, simply smile!

Smiling;

*Makes you happy, even when there is no one around.
*When someone is around you put them at ease.
*Tells other people that you are approachable.
*Smiling at others almost always brings smiles back to you.
*It costs you nothing to bring joy to others.

On Being a Hero

Many people dream of being a hero. Saving a child from a burning building, rescuing a drowning person or foiling a robbery. Given the opportunity, why not do all three!

If none of these situations or other heroic situations don't present themselves you can still be a renowned hero to everyone you meet by doing simple acts of kindness.

1. Open the door for others.
2. Help carry groceries.
3. Buy candy (or popcorn, cookies, candles, etc.) from every young person that comes to your door, even when you don't need what they are selling. (That's what "re-gifting" is for.)
4. Stop and help some one that has car trouble or is stuck in the snow.
5. Do more than you are asked and ask more of yourself than you do of others.
6. Help someone you don't know that has no way of "paying you back".
7. It is easy to be pleasant to the pretty, the handsome, the young, the rich or the popular. Be just as pleasant to those that are not.
8. Volunteer to help on a project, *before* you are asked to volunteer.

9. Help a budding entrepreneur! When you see a lemonade stand stop and buy a drink even if you are not thirsty. An extra special gift to the child running the lemonade stand would be to congratulate them on their gumption to try and run a business.

10. Give away a certain amount (say 10%) of every dollar you earn to those less fortunate. This will build your confidence.

11. Always remember that it is impossible to give more than you receive.

Whispering

When I was in college one beautiful spring day, I stopped to visit (and perhaps ask out) one of the prettiest girls on campus. After a few minutes of idle chatter, I was about to pop the all important question about "Friday night", when a bird, high above decided to "poop" on my shoulder.

From that day, until she graduated two years later, it seemed whenever she saw me, she was whispering and laughing. Maybe it was just me. Maybe I was still embarrassed. Maybe she was laughing at me. Maybe she wasn't. All I know is that I *felt* she was laughing at me.

If you are speaking in front of a group of people or even a bunch of your friends, and out of the corner of your eye you see someone whispering (and/or laughing) it is a very uncomfortable feeling. It's like, well...a bird just "pooped" on your shoulder.

Borrowing

It is best not to borrow money from a friend or family member. It has been my experience when I have loaned money to a "friend" I have usually lost either the friend, the money or both. Borrowing money from a family member can really take the fun out of family dinners and holiday gatherings. If you must borrow money, go to the bank. That is why they are in business.

As for borrowing "things", the best rule of thumb is to return the item in better condition than when you borrowed it. Several times I have had to borrow a neighbor's pick-up truck to make a run to the dump, pick up a piece of furniture or haul some equipment to the repair shop. Everytime, I borrow his truck, I return it full of gas and freshly washed. For some reason, everytime I ask to borrow the truck my neighbor is very happy to loan it to me. As with most things in life, getting what you had hoped for is achieved simply by doing more than expected.

Quote

You don't have to be a famous person, movie star or author to say something smart or clever. Anyone can come up with a great idea or saying that is worth repeating.

However, give credit where credit is due. If you are repeating something that you heard or read, don't pass it off as your own, unless of course it is your own. This is especially true if you are quoting someone you know.

If you use someone's idea or saying without giving them credit you have stolen something of value from that person. Stealing is wrong. Enough said.

Let 'em In

My dad passed away in the year 2000. He was a wonderful man, except for being a very rude driver. He would never let another driver "in" if they were in the "wrong" lane or trying to move out of a crowded parking lot. However when he was in the "wrong" lane, or trying to get out of a crowded parking lot, he would always shake his head and sigh, "Ah, they just never give you a break".

Sometimes when we are driving, we are in the wrong lane. Or we may be in a huge shopping center parking lot trying to leave when the traffic is the thickest. You've been there on both sides. Sometimes, you're in the "wrong" lane, and sometimes you're in the "right" lane when someone else is trying to get in. Let 'em in. You'll brighten their day and yours with this simple, free act of kindness.

P.S. If you are the person being "let in", be sure to give that little "wave". It is a way of saying thank you for the other persons kindness toward you.

Explaining/Complaining

Growing up I was taught "A gentleman doesn't explain and a gentleman does not complain". In other words, if you are late, you are late. You don't "explain" you were late because the traffic was bad, you had a flat tire or your mother ate your homework again. You don't complain, "that's not fair that I don't get to "start the game" (or get the promotion), because I was late".

In other words you are responsible for your actions. Period.

Don't be a Fig, Remember Dates

Use a calendar of some sort and write down the important dates that you need to remember. Birthdays, anniversaries, graduations, holidays, etc. are opportunities to show that you are thinking of someone besides yourself. (It is a strange phenomenon, that the more you think of others, the more they think of you. The more you think of yourself, the less other people think of you.)

A huge number of people either forget an important date for a friend or family member or they send something belated. A divorced father I know sent his 10 year old daughter a stunning gold watch for her birthday in September. The only problem was her birthday was in May. How do you think she felt? How would you feel?

Remembering important dates shows that you are organized, caring and you are thinking about others. Other people will notice.

Let 'em In, Part 2

Have you ever had to run to the store for a certain item you needed for school, or bread to make sandwiches for tomorrow's work or school. You've run in the store, found the item you need, head to the check-out area and the only checker that is open, has a shopper in front of you stocking up for Noah's Ark.

Let's just hope that Noah's shopper takes a tip from kind driver's of the road and let's you in. It is simply the right thing to do.

Dating

My two older brothers and myself were separated in age by 2 ½ years. Hence we shared almost everything. For a time we only had one bike, which we of course shared. One brother would ride the bike while the other two brothers ran along side. We all slept in a 10 X 12 foot bedroom with one very small closet. Because we were all about the same size we shared the same clothes. (The shirts and pants were a little bit small for the oldest, a little bit big for the youngest, but fit the middle brother just right).

When we got to high school and started dating we were taught the "Gentleman's Rules of Dating". It does not matter if you are 16 or 60, the "rules" still apply.

1. One must always ask for a date a reasonable amount of time before the planned date.
2. The "date" must be planned.
    A. Where you are going
    B. What time you will pick up your date
    C. What time you plan to bring your date home.
3. When you pick up your date, you should always go to your date's front door, knock, introduce yourself to her parents or roommates, (or, if you are older, maybe her children).

4. It is the responsibility of _both_ people to make sure that it is an enjoyable date for both parties.

5. Whether it is the first date or the fortieth date a gentleman always walks his date to her door at the end of the date.

6. Everyone wants to feel special. Why not send your date flowers, or a humorous card _before the date,_ saying how much you are looking forward to your time together. For the female, a small box of home made chocolate chip cookies for when your date arrives to pick you up, says that you are thinking about someone besides yourself. When I was younger a certain girl would always give me _ChapStick_ when ever I picked her up for our date. That was both thoughful and encouraging!

7. Finally in the beginning of this section I talked about how close my older brothers and myself were and how we shared _almost_ everything. What my brothers and myself _never_ shared with each other, or for that matter anyone else, was the mental or physical part of the date. A gentleman (or a lady) never discloses with anyone else what was discussed on a date (such as a person's secrets, worries or goals), and _never ever anything of a physical nature_ that went on during the date. To do so is childish, rude, and shows a total disrespect and compassion for your date. For goodness sakes grow up!

Please

"Please" is an interesting word. By saying "please" to a person you are inferring that they have the power to say "yes" or "no". Everyone likes power and everyone likes a person that says "please".

"Please" is only used for asking, never for begging or whining.

Thank You

You can never say "thank you" too many times. My youngest daughter will often say "thank you" three or four times for taking her to the store, over to a friends house, out for a hamburger or helping her with a project. I never get tired of hearing it.

I'm Sorry

Have you ever noticed how difficult it is to have another person continue to be mad at you if you continue to say a very heart felt "I'm sorry"?

For instance say that you broke your mother's favorite salad bowl that has been in the family for generations. The conversation would probably go something like this:

(Mom) "I can't believe you broke my favorite salad bowl".

(Son/Daughter) "Mom, I am so sorry"

(Mom) "That bowl has been in the family since great grandpa owned the largest buggy whip factory in the world"

(Son/Daughter) "I know that was an important family memento, I am so sorry I broke it, Mom.

(Mom) "Well, I am sad that you broke it, but I know it was an accident"

(Son/Daughter) "Accident or not it is still broken and I am truly sorry"

(Mom) "It's really not that important. I don't want you to feel bad"

Remember you can be sorry without saying you are wrong. For instance, if you have had an argument with a friend that was suppose to pick you up, and (you believe) they forgot, and (they believe) they never agreed to pick you up. Rather than continuing to try to convince them that they are wrong (which is hard to do), and they try to convince you that you are wrong (maybe even harder to do). You simply say, "I am sorry we've had this disagreement". You have not agreed that they are right or that you are wrong. What you have done is decided that on the grand scale of life no matter who is at fault, blame is not going to be resolved and is not as important as your friendship.

As a point of reference "sorry" is only healing when it is spoken with kindness and feeling. To put extra stress on the last syllable, as in "sor-reeeey" changes a word of truce to a word that invites battle.

Fowl (Foul) Language
is for the Birds

Sometime around the third or fourth grade some of the "tougher" kids let slip a couple of "swear words" just to show how "mature" they really are, even though their mother still drives them to school, makes their lunch and coddles them at home like a baby. As time goes on, even the "good kids" start to go with the crowd and "salt" their language with a few choice words. By Jr. High School, most gatherings of these early teenagers sound like a rough day on an oil rig or your Dad after he mashed his finger hanging a picture for your Mom, when all he wanted to do is watch the game on TV.

It is interesting to note that as we all age, there is no class or educational distinction between those that "do" and those that "don't" use the limited appeal of swear words to convey their thoughts and emotions.

Points to Ponder:

1. Is everyone comfortable when you use foul language?
2. Is everyone comfortable if you don't use foul language?
3. Why do you think you have to "swear"?
4. When you are an adult, would you like your children to "swear".
5. Is the use of foul language the only way you can convey your thoughts and opinions?

A Personal Confession on the Use of Profanity

Like most kids growing up I easily slipped into swearing when I was around "the guys". Although I know both males and females swear a blue streak today, when I was younger girls didn't swear, and most guys did not swear when they were in the presence of females.

In my late 20's, for no particular reason and certainly not relying on any moral conviction a thought came to me. Everyone I knew to some extent used foul language to express themselves. Why not be different and try to completely remove all swear words from all my communications?

It would be a falsehood to say that I never uttered a swear word from that day on. I did however, get to the point where it was a real rarity when any a swear word slipped out. In fact I cleaned up my language so much that if I were speaking to a female and _she_ said a swear word, it was often followed with her saying "excuse me".

Then I took up golf.

Being a Polite Well Mannered Person is Simple

About 20 years ago the football coach Lou Holtz did a short film titled, <u>Do Right!</u>

At the time Coach Holtz was coach of the #1 ranked football team, *The Fighting Irish* of Notre Dame. In the film he talked about how building a champion football team is no different than building a champion business team, a champion family team or a person that is a champion.

His three main points were;

1. Do what is right.
2. Do your best.
3. Do unto others as you would have them do unto you, (sometimes referred to as *The Golden Rule*.)

Is it right to chew with your mouth open, wear your hat indoors or interrupt?

Are you at your "best" when you gossip, lie, cheat or steal?

How would you like to be treated? Do you like to wait for people who are late? When you're in front of the room, giving a talk, how do you feel when people are whispering to one another while you're trying to speak?

These were the three rules we used raising our two daughters. When you think about it, they pretty much cover all bases.

In short, having good manners is simple, but rare. Having good manners sets you apart from the crowd. Having good manners does not cost a thing, but it will make you one in a million.

"Be the change that you want to see in the world".
Mohandas Gandhi

www.ingramcontent.com/pod-product-compliance
Lightning Source LLC
Chambersburg PA
CBHW071250280526
45788CB00004B/1657